This book belongs to:

_____

Look and See

Donna McMillan

Vander Publishing House

Reginald and Tevin McMillan Cover Designer

Reginald McMillan Graphics Designer

LOOK AND SEE

Donna McMillan

Vander Publishing House

Look at the farm
and what do you see?

Cows

pigs

ponies

and a yellow chick-a-dee!

Look in the yard
and what do you see?

Cats

dogs

squirrels

and rabbits!
Can't you see?

Look at the zoo
and what do you see?

Zebras

bears

tigers

and a monkey in the tree!

Look in the ocean
and what do you see?

Fish

whales

dolphins

and a seahorse for me!

Look in the sky
and what do you see?

Butterflies

birds

and bumble bees!

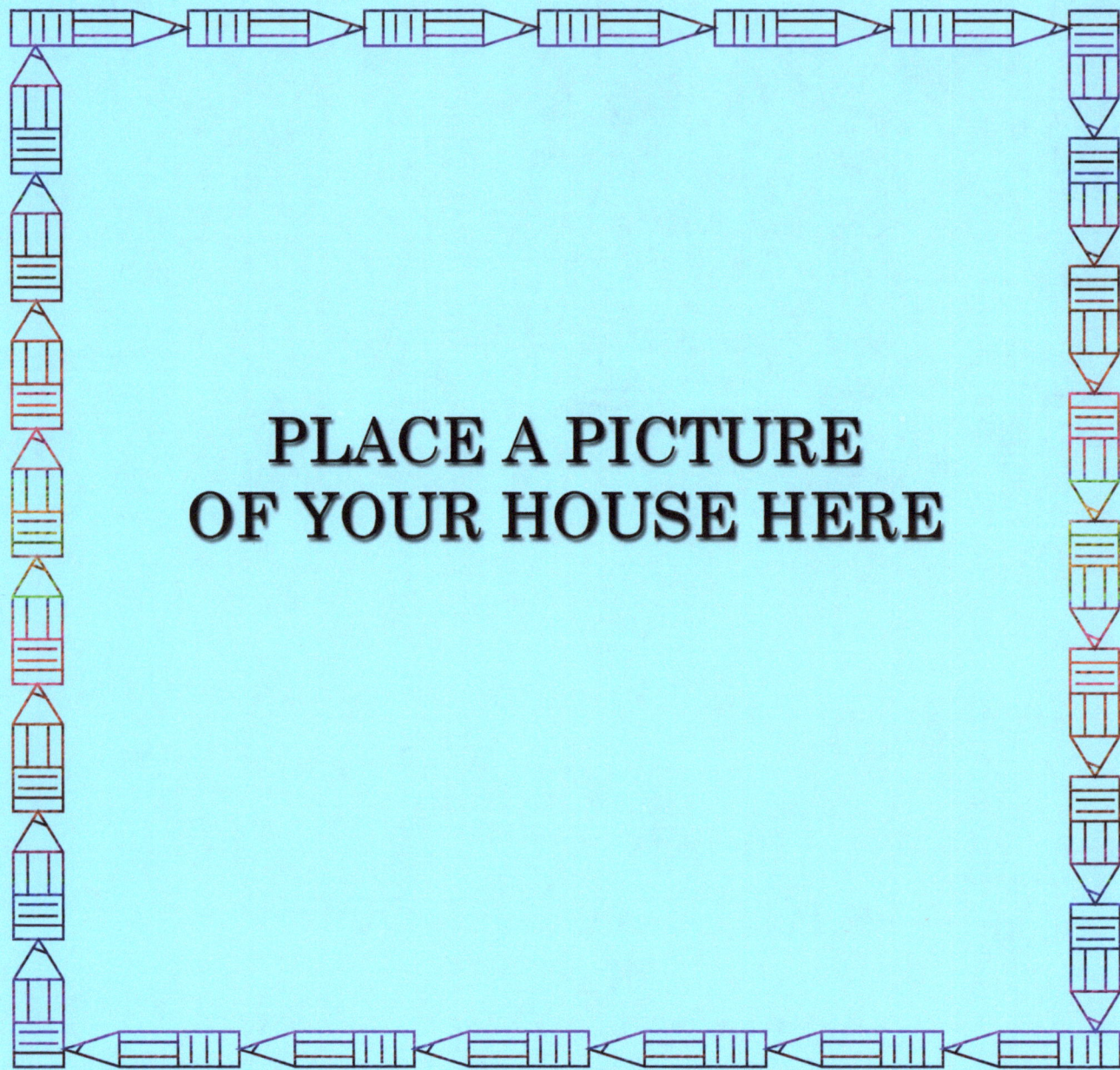

PLACE A PICTURE
OF YOUR HOUSE HERE

Look in the house and
what do you see?

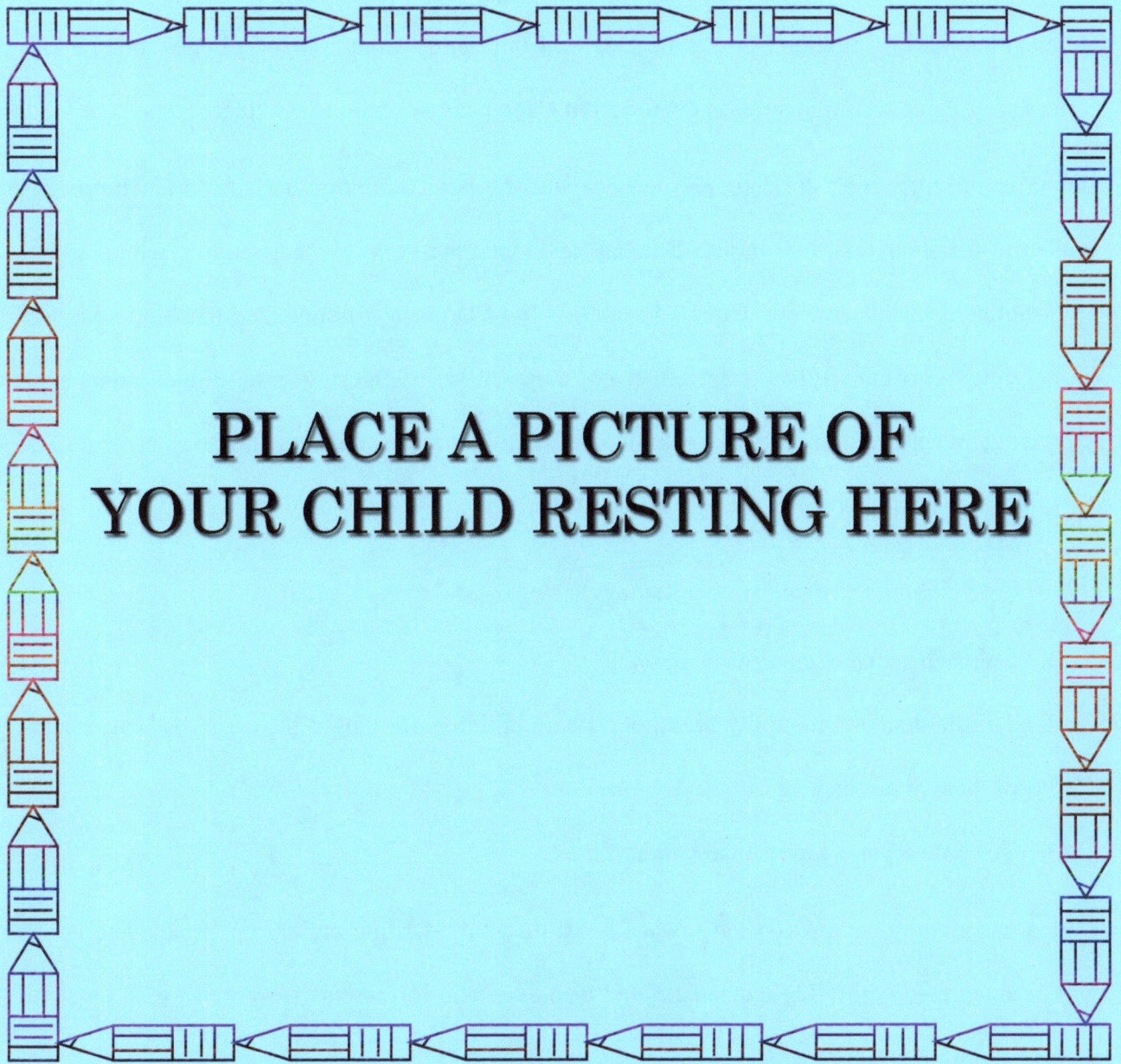

PLACE A PICTURE OF
YOUR CHILD RESTING HERE

A bed for tired, tired me!

Given the right tools at the right time, no child will be left behind. This is the philosophy of Donna M. McMillan, a passionate, dedicated, and determined Early Childhood Education teacher. Donna was born and raised in the port city, Wilmington, North Carolina, where she obtained her Early Childhood Education Degree from Stanly Community College, and she also earned her Business Administration degree from Cape Fear Community College, respectively.

Donna is currently a pre-kindergarten teacher and she has committed her life to teaching each student to reach beyond their limits. She has developed her very own curriculum, which allows her to implement this concept. Parents speak highly of Donnas' personalized teaching style and of how her curriculum has contributed to their children entering into kindergarten with knowledge beyond that expected of a kindergartener. Donna ensures that she gives each student the tools they need to become not only successful students, but individuals as well.

Donna has several goals in life:

1. To reach as many children as possible.
2. To establish a community preschool where children are taught beyond what is expected of them at an early age.
3. To write several educational children books.

Donna has already begun working toward her third goal—writing children's books. The books will be integrated within her curriculum and also available for parents who aren't able to enroll their child into her program.

Ordinary preschool becomes extraordinary learning with Donna. She's truly mastered turning preschool education into a stepping stone for children to advance their knowledge and gain a true head-start in life!

www.ingramcontent.com/pod-product-compliance
Lightning Source LLC
Chambersburg PA
CBHW041555040426

42447CB00002B/181

LOOK AND SEE

Animals are an important part of life. In **LOOK AND SEE** children are introduced to different animals and the places in which they live. This is an excellent book for children up to five years old.

Tiger obtained from Wallpaper2background.com

ISBN 9780615871806

90000

9 780615 871806